I0801068

IMAGES
of America

Bath Iron Works

A Bath Iron Works (BIW) mechanic poses *c.* 1920 with a reduction gear fabricated in the Machine Shop. This gear was built for the collier *Thomas P. Beal*, Bath Iron Works hull No. 86, delivered to Crowell & Thurlow shipping in 1921. For many years, the yard constructed the propulsion machinery for its ships, in addition to building engines for external customers.

On the cover: Guided missile frigates *Harry E. Yarnell* (DLG 17) and *Worden* (DLG 18) are seen fitting out at the yard's north pier on January 2, 1963. These frigates were typical of guided missile warships built at Bath in the 1960s. Each carried 80 anti-aircraft missiles in launchers fore and aft, plus an eight-cell launcher for anti-submarine rockets. These ships served the Navy into the 1990s.

IMAGES
of America

BATH IRON WORKS

Andrew C. Toppan

ARCADIA
PUBLISHING

ISBN 978-0-7385-1059-0

Published by Arcadia Publishing
Charleston, South Carolina

Printed in the United States of America

Library of Congress Catalog Card Number: 2002107335

For all general information contact Arcadia Publishing at:
Telephone 843-853-2070
Fax 843-853-0044
E-mail sales@arcadiapublishing.com
For customer service and orders:
Toll-Free 1-888-313-2665

Visit us on the Internet at www.arcadiapublishing.com

The destroyer *Knapp* (DD 653), Bath Iron Works hull No. 218, is ready for launch from the north ways on July 10, 1943. Bath is at the peak of its wartime mass-production program, averaging one destroyer delivery every 17 days. At least a dozen ships are in various stages of construction in the shipyard on any given day.

CONTENTS

ACKNOWLEDGMENTS

This book would not have been possible without the assistance of Bath Iron Works. All photographs not otherwise credited are courtesy of Bath Iron Works, drawn from the company's photograph archive. Communications department director Sue Pierter and her staff—Gayle Stodder, Stephen Cote, Candy Summers, and Sarah Turgeon—were all gracious and helpful in accommodating my research for the book. Thanks also go to Paul Silverstone, William S. Bailey, Brian Bailey, Craig Pulver, and Ron Bartlett for providing other photographs to supplement the yard's archives. Special thanks also go to the many folks at Bath Iron Works who contributed experiences and recollections from their shipbuilding careers, providing many interesting anecdotes to bring history to life.

Many published references were consulted for historical information. Most important was Ralph Linwood Snow's comprehensive history *Bath Iron Works: The First Hundred Years*. Garnett Laidlaw Eskew's 1958 *Cradle of Ships* also proved useful, along with Bath Iron Work's internal *List of Ships*, compiled by Mark Cheetham, Department 55, and the U.S. Navy's *Dictionary of American Naval Fighting Ships* for histories of Bath's warships. A variety of Bath Iron Works publications, including annual reports, promotional and marketing pamphlets, and launch day programs, were also consulted.

Guided missile destroyers *John King* (DDG 3) and *Sampson* are pictured at the north pier in January 1961. *John King* is just days from delivery to the Navy, while *Sampson* will follow in six months. The ships' profiles are reminiscent of the wartime destroyers built 20 years earlier, but they bristle with modern electronics and carry a missile launcher aft.

Introduction

In 1607, the settlers at Popham Colony, at the mouth of the Kennebec River, launched a 50-foot sailing pinnace. Named *Virginia*, the pinnace was the first seagoing ship built by settlers in America. Thus Popham, the Kennebec River, and modern-day Bath, Maine, became the birthplace of shipbuilding in America. Nearly four centuries later, Bath Iron Works still builds ships on the Kennebec, 12 miles upstream from Popham, carrying on the region's shipbuilding tradition. In the intervening years, the river has been home to hundreds of shipyards that produced thousands of ships. Ships built in and around Bath have been big and small, famous and unnoticed, long-lived or doomed to an early demise. They have included full-rigged sailing ships, schooners, barges, freighters, tankers, tugs, yachts, warships, and more. Today, when a sleek new destroyer leaves Bath Iron Works, sailing down the Kennebec and past Fort Popham at the river's mouth, it carries the legacy of four centuries of shipbuilding.

Since its incorporation in 1884, Bath Iron Works is best known as a builder of naval vessels. The yard's association with the Navy began with Bath Iron Works hull No. 2, the gunboat USS *Machias*, delivered in 1893. A few years later, Bath started building torpedo boats for the Navy, the predecessors to the destroyers that later became the yard's mainstay. When the nation went to war, Bath Iron Works went to work, turning out a dozen fast destroyers as part of the World War I shipbuilding program. Although torpedo boats and destroyers dominated Bath's work for the Navy, there were other naval ships too—a bizarre armored ram, gunboats, a coast defense monitor, a training ship, two cruisers, and a massive battleship, plus lightships for the U.S. Light House Service.

The early years at Bath Iron Works were not completely occupied with government ships, however. The yard turned out a wide variety of commercial and privately owned vessels. They ranged from tugs and barges to freighters, passenger steamers, ferries, yachts, small sailing craft, and the racing sloop *Defiance*, defender of the America's Cup. This commercial work helped fill the gaps between warship orders, but was not enough to keep the shipyard going when Navy orders dried up after World War I. With no new orders in sight, Bath Iron Works was forced into liquidation in 1925.

In 1927, Pete Newell, a former manager at the yard, obtained a lease on the shipyard property and reincorporated Bath Iron Works. The yard started out building trawlers and yachts and was soon launching immense yachts, such as *Hi-Esmaro*, *Corsair IV*, *Aras*, and *Caroline*, among the largest of their era. *Ranger* was the yard's second America's Cup defender and one of the most famous ships built at Bath. Trawlers, yachts, and Coast Guard cutters carried the yard into the late 1930s, when destroyer orders from the Navy began to pick up again. In 1940, the yard began a massive expansion project to prepare for World War II shipbuilding and was well rewarded with destroyer orders. During the war, Bath Iron Works delivered some 82 destroyers—one quarter of the Navy's destroyer fleet and more destroyers than the entire Japanese navy constructed during the same time.

In the postwar years, Bath Iron Works has continued to excel in naval shipbuilding, delivering dozens of destroyers, escorts, frigates, and cruisers over the years. Complementing the naval work has been a variety of commercial work, from trawlers to tankers. Today, the yard is constructing modern *Arleigh Burke*-class *Aegis* guided missile destroyers. Bath Iron Works is also planning for the next generation of destroyers to carry the shipyard and the Navy into the 21st century. With modernized facilities and a skilled workforce, Bath Iron Works is well positioned to continue its long legacy of shipbuilding.

Space does not permit a full listing of the shipyard's construction record, so a brief summary will suffice. In 119 years, Bath Iron Works has built 410 vessels, ranging from a 15-foot motor launch to a 720-foot container ship. Two hundred twenty-nine of the ships were for the U.S.

Navy, 21 for other branches of government, and 3 for the German navy. One hundred three ships were for commercial owners, 52 were yachts for private owners, and 1 was for Bath's own use. Nearly all the naval vessels—212 of the 229—were destroyers, their variants, or predecessors, including frigates, destroyer escorts, and guided missile cruisers. Half of the commercial ships were trawlers; the others ranged from barges and tugs to container ships. The 52 yachts included everything from small launches to sailing schooners, up to 300-foot superyachts, such as J.P. Morgan's magnificent *Corsair IV*. Twenty-two of the yachts, 14 of the trawlers, and 16 commercial ships later saw service in the Navy or Army, totaling 305 ships for the armed forces.

This book illustrates not only the ships but also the shipyard and the shipbuilders. Many of the photographs show the shipbuilding process, both in the shops and on the ways, in addition to some of the non-shipboard products built by BIW over the years. The book is arranged into the general eras of BIW's history, as defined by the major events and transitions in the projects. Within each chapter, the photographs are generally arranged chronologically and grouped in terms of the yard's major projects and events. This arrangement, and the use of many interesting or unusual photographs, will tell the story of the ships, shipyard, and the proud shipbuilders of Bath.

Members of the Bath Iron Works operating crew pose with the frigate *Klakring* in Bath's elderly wooden drydock. Built prior to World War I and thus older than the men in the photograph, the dock was acquired in 1976, providing BIW with on-site drydocking facilities for the first time. Construction of 24 frigates like *Klakring* was one of Bath's largest and most successful shipbuilding programs, earning the slogan "ahead of schedule and under budget."

One

The Early Years: Birth of a Shipyard

The first ships built at Bath Iron Works, and the first steel vessels built in Maine, were the Navy gunboats *Machias* (right) and *Castine*. Their keels were laid on February 4, 1891, and this view shows their construction progressed by a few months. The yard is small and simple but will soon grow into a major shipbuilding facility. Bath's shops are to the right; residential areas lie uphill. For more than 110 years, the yard's shipways, the center of shipbuilding operations, occupied this same spot on the riverbank.

Gen. Thomas Worcester Hyde, a native of Bath, purchased the Bath Iron Foundry, a successful local business, upon his return from war in 1865. In 1884, he renamed the company Bath Iron Works, Limited, and four years later acquired the defunct Goss Marine Iron Works located nearby. This new property gave BIW a waterfront location suitable for shipbuilding, and a new shipyard was born.

Before expanding into shipbuilding, the foundry's business was centered on the Hyde Windlass and other shipboard machinery. The original deck machinery business was spun off as Hyde Windlass Company in 1896, relocating to the former Morse shipyard, just downstream from Bath's yard. Hyde Windlass was reacquired by Bath Iron Works in 1961, and its facilities were later incorporated into the growing shipyard.

Bath Iron Works hull No. 1 was the coastal steamer *Cottage City*, delivered in 1890. Ironically, it was a wooden ship, and construction of the hull was subcontracted to another shipyard. Bath built and installed the machinery and completed the outfitting of the vessel. Several early Bath Iron Works contracts for wooden-hulled vessels were handled by similar subcontracts.

The gunboat *Machias* is at the pier following sea trials. The yard's shops lie astern and behind the ship. On trials, *Machias* reached 15.46 knots, easily exceeding the contract speed of 14 knots. *Machias* and *Castine* introduced the Navy to BIW and started a long relationship that continues today. After 27 years with the U.S. Navy, *Machias* was sold to Mexico and served until 1935.

The unique armored ram *Katahdin* slips into the Kennebec on February 4, 1893. Built as part of a planned coast defense network, it was meant to sink enemy ships by ramming, hence the sharp, beak-like bow. The low-profile hull was a form of 19th-century stealth. Due to design problems beyond Bath's control, *Katahdin* could not meet the contract speed, and BIW spent a great deal of money trying to fix the problem. This included construction of a floating cofferdam so the propeller could be replaced while the ship was afloat.

Katahdin demonstrates its low profile at sea—a feature that left its decks awash in anything but a flat calm. With a change in administrations, the Navy realized the ship's shortcomings and tried to refuse delivery, threatening the yard's survival. Congress eventually took action to get payment for Bath, and the Navy let *Katahdin* languish at the pier for several years before using the ram as a gunnery target. (Photograph courtesy author's collection.)

Even before the *Katahdin* debacle, the new shipyard faced another challenge. Early on the morning of February 13, 1894, in the midst of a blizzard, a massive fire swept through BIW. The city mains could not supply enough water to control the flames, and virtually all of the shipyard's buildings were destroyed. The yacht *Eleanor* was on the shipways and escaped with minor damage, but a large steam windlass under construction for another shipyard was ruined. Losses were estimated at $140,000, and General Hyde threatened to leave Bath forever but eventually decided to rebuild the yard. The photograph above looks northeast, toward the river. The shipbuilding ways are out of view to the right; the Machine Shop is the large building to the left. The view below was taken inside one of the ruined shops.

The 220-foot steam-and-sail yacht *Eleanor* was on the ways when the 1894 fire struck, but it survived with minor damage. When completed later that year, *Eleanor* was the largest yacht in the United States, and the owner celebrated with a 17-month world cruise. The elegant yacht served the Navy as a patrol ship during World War I. *Eleanor* was the first in a long line of yachts built at Bath Iron Works. (Photograph courtesy author's collection.)

Although yacht-like in appearance and remarkably similar to *Eleanor*'s dimensions, the gunboat *Newport* was intended as a warship from the start. *Newport* was delivered in 1897 and saw action along with its Bath-built sister *Vicksburg* in the Spanish-American War. The era of sail warships quickly passed, and *Newport* served mainly as a training ship after 1900. (Photograph courtesy author's collection.)

Over the years, Bath Iron Works built many smaller vessels indoors. Here, the torpedo boat *T.A.M. Craven* stands ready for launch from the newly expanded Plate Shop in 1899. The Plate Shop was the yard's largest building, constructed in the post-fire rebuilding and expanded for construction of *Craven* and sister *Dahlgren*. Torpedo boats were built for speed—*Craven* exceeded 31 knots on trials, a virtually unheard-of speed at the time.

This unique shiphouse was built in 1898 to accommodate construction of yachts too large to fit in the Plate Shop. Protection from the weather was important during Maine's cold winters. In this view, two hulls are barely visible on the ways north of the shiphouse. The blacksmith shop is in the foreground at the western boundary of the shipyard.

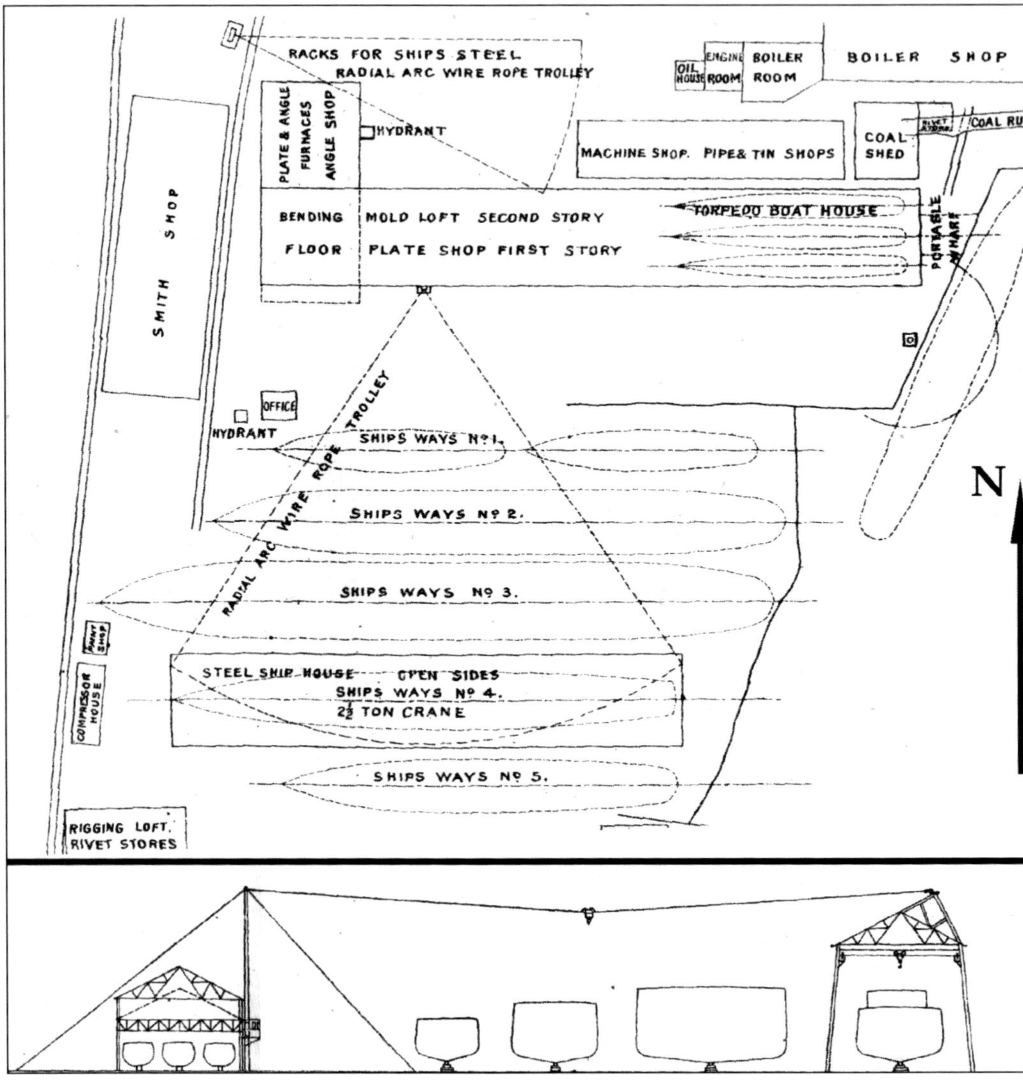

This plan and profile view of the shipyard dates from the turn of the century. There were a total of five major shipways, including one under the shiphouse. Each way could accommodate a single large ship, or two smaller vessels end-to-end. The Plate Shop had its own set of ways and could accommodate up to three torpedo boats, although the boats had to be shifted sideways from their building positions onto a single set of ways prior to launch. The yard lacked the normal heavy cranes, instead using a cable-suspended overhead trolley system, somewhat like a modern ski lift. The system was supported by the curved monorail on the shiphouse roof. There was a heavy-lift derrick at the fitting-out pier, where boilers and engines were installed. (Photograph courtesy author's collection.)

Col. Oliver H. Payne chartered Bath's grand yacht *Eleanor* soon after its completion and promptly decided to order a larger version for himself. The product was the 330-foot *Aphrodite*, delivered in 1899 and described as a "sea palace" of incomparable luxury. The yacht was ruggedly built, meant for all-weather worldwide cruising. While serving the Navy during World War I, the yacht hit a mine but survived the explosion.

Aphrodite is pierside at BIW, repainted gray since the sea trials photograph. Two coastal steamers undergoing maintenance lie astern. *Aphrodite* was the first vessel constructed in the shiphouse. The shiphouse lies beyond the yacht's rigging; the yard's heavy derrick is at the far right. Both *Aphrodite* and *Eleanor* were under Greek ownership in the 1920s, operating as passenger ferries.

In sharp contrast to *Aphrodite*'s stately grandeur was the humble coast defense monitor *Nevada*, delivered in 1903. Like the earlier *Katahdin*, *Nevada* was an ill-conceived ship, with a low freeboard that rendered seagoing service impractical. Along with three sisters, the ship was later outfitted as a support ship for submarines. *Nevada*'s low decks were a perfect match for submarines, but its two 12-inch guns were never put to good use.

A group of Bath Iron Works employees pose for a photograph during the yard's early years. This appears to be the new Machine Shop, constructed in 1898 and 1899 to replace an outdated 1882 structure. To keep production moving while the new building was constructed, it was built around the old shop, which was then demolished. The Machine Shop was the center of the shipyard's operations for decades and is the oldest major building in the yard today.

Georgia, Bath's only battleship, towers over the shipyard on launch day, October 11, 1904. At 441 feet long and over 16,000 tons full load, *Georgia* was the largest Bath-built ship until the commercial ships of the late 1960s. Perhaps the ship was too much for Bath's facilities—the yard had considerable trouble handling the heavy armor and four 12-inch guns. Unlike *Nevada*, however, *Georgia* was a fast, seaworthy, and capable ship.

After five years under construction, *Georgia* goes to sea. One year after commissioning, the battleship joined the round-the-world cruise of the Navy's battle fleet, known as the Great White Fleet. In addition to the main battery of 12-inch guns, *Georgia* carried eight 8-inch and twelve 6-inch guns, plus 24 light guns and 4 underwater torpedo tubes.

A smaller, faster counterpart to *Georgia* was the scout cruiser *Chester*. This June 26, 1907 view finds the cruiser ready for launch, with the sponsor's platform and ceremonial bunting in place. *Chester* was the first Navy ship with steam turbine engines instead of the traditional reciprocating engines and exceeded 26.5 knots on trials. Two similar ships built at another shipyard had different engines. In competitive trials, *Chester* came out on top, proving the new technology's worth.

As the shipbuilding business grew, Bath Iron Works continued building engines for its ships and for outside customers. This engine is for the Bath-built steamer *Moosehead*, delivered to the Maine Central Railroad in 1911. Reciprocating engines such as this one remained popular for many years, even as the Navy switched to turbines in high-performance ships such as *Chester*.

Two

The Destroyer Years: World War I Comes to Bath

Flusser, the first destroyer built at Bath Iron Works, slides into the Kennebec River on July 20, 1909, as smoke rises from the ways. Destroyers, descendants of the earlier torpedo boats, were the bulk of the yard's business during the pre–World War I military buildup and well into the postwar years. Nearly five times heavier than the torpedo boat *T.A.M. Craven*, and with engines six times as powerful, the 293-foot *Flusser* surpassed 33 knots on sea trials.

Flusser's speed can be attributed to its revolutionary steam turbine engines, the first fitted in any Navy destroyer. Here one of *Flusser*'s turbines sits, cover open, in the yard's Machine Shop prior to installation. The turbines were precisely machined pieces of equipment, built by Bath under license from the turbine design companies—in this case Parsons Marine Steam Turbine Company of Wallsend-on-Tyne, England.

This is a view of *Flusser*'s completed engine room. A forest of steam pipes converges on the central control station, with its collection of gauges and control wheels. The turbines themselves lie below deck level in the foreground. While the engine room looks pleasant enough in this dockside view, it is a hot and noisy place when the ship is under way.

Before the engines were installed in the ships, they were completely assembled and checked out in the Machine Shop. *Flusser's* plant was in a three-shaft configuration, with five turbines using and reusing steam at successively lower pressures to gain the greatest efficiency. The five turbines could be connected in several combinations for different speed requirements. Turbine engines such as these were far more efficient than earlier reciprocating engines, far more powerful, and they vibrated less. The turbines were powered by four steam boilers—*Flusser's* boilers were being assembled in Bath's Boiler Shop when that building burned down in 1908, delaying completion of the ship. The Boiler Shop was the last remaining building from the old Goss Marine Iron Works.

This *c.* 1910 view of the shipyard looks south over Maine Central Railroad yards. The big Machine Shop building dominates the view, with the shiphouse roof and monorail appearing in the distance; the pier and derrick are to the left. The land immediately north of the shop, the former Union Wharf property, was purchased by BIW in 1909, providing space for a new foundry building.

This view looks down the main bay of the Machine Shop in 1910 toward the east (river) end. Like the earlier Plate Shop, the Machine Shop could accommodate indoor construction of ships. The shop has two overhead cranes, and a railroad track passes through the shop in the foreground. To the left are condensers for a destroyer's steam plant.

The destroyer *Drayton* is on sea trials in 1910. The guns, provided by the Navy, will be installed after delivery; weights were temporarily installed in their place for trials. By 1910, oil was starting to replace coal as a fuel—*Drayton* was the second oil-fired destroyer built at Bath and only the third oil-fired ship in the Navy.

Destroyers *Cummins* and *Cassin* are pictured at the yard's pier in 1913, the year they were launched and delivered. *Cassin* was torpedoed in 1917 and lost its stern; repairs took six months. These destroyers lasted just over 20 years, scrapped in 1934 after several years as Coast Guard patrol ships during Prohibition.

The destroyer *Wadsworth*, delivered in 1915, introduced reduction gears to the Navy. The marine equivalent of a transmission, the gears connect the steam turbines, which are most efficient at high speeds, to the propellers, which are most efficient when spinning slowly. The result is greatly improved efficiency. *Wadsworth*'s gears were considered revolutionary in their day.

In contrast to *Wadsworth*'s modern machinery, 1915 also saw delivery of *Emblane*, a torpedo trials vessel. *Emblane* was powered by this traditional vertical triple expansion (VTE) reciprocating steam engine, which produced 215 horsepower. The engine was, naturally, Bath-built. In this view, the engine sits on the outfitting pier before being installed in the ship.

Scattered among the destroyers were a number of commercial vessels and yachts. *Katahdin* was constructed at Bath, dismantled, shipped overland to Moosehead Lake, and reassembled in 1914. The steamer towed logs for the timber industry until 1975 and, in 1985, was restored and returned to service as an excursion ship, as seen here. *Katahdin* is Bath's oldest known operating Bath-built vessel. Built as hull No. 63, it carries the number proudly on its bow.

Winchester was a fast commuter yacht delivered in 1916. Like the destroyers of the time, it sported turbine engines. The yacht's speed proved valuable as a warship, and *Winchester* served the U.S. Navy during World War I and the Canadian navy during World War II. Another big, fast commuter yacht of this era, *Isabel*, was considered a destroyer when taken into the Navy.

The destroyer *Manley*, seen on trials, was a prototype for the flush decker destroyers that would become the standard design for World War I and postwar construction. Numerically the last of the six prototypes, *Manley* was the first one completed—less than two months after launching. Although built in wartime haste, *Manley* had a long life.

In 1939, *Manley* became a prototype again—the first of many older destroyers converted to fast troop transports to carry raiding forces. Half the boilers and much of the armament were removed, replaced by four landing craft and space for troops and their equipment. *Manley* was the second-oldest destroyer in the fleet during World War II—the oldest was another Bath-built ship, *Allen*. (Photograph courtesy Paul Silverstone.)

The flush decker *Wickes* is nearly obscured by wooden staging on the ways c. 1917. The ship was the first of 11 flush deckers built at Bath and the first of 273 built throughout the country. The Navy prepared the basic design for these ships and then had Bath and Bethlehem Steel prepare separate detailed designs. Bethlehem's three shipyards built to their design, but the seven other shipyards, including the Navy's, worked to the Bath design. The Bath design was considered superior, and the Bath-designed ships generally lasted longer.

Wickes, shown during World War I, wears camouflage paint. The ship was in service for only four years before being laid up in reserve. In 1940, *Wickes* became HMS *Montgomery*, one of 50 destroyers transferred to the United Kingdom in the early days of World War II. The old ships were a stopgap measure, but they served well until newer ships arrived to replace them.

When the wartime destroyer contracts were completed, Bath Iron Works found other work, such as the collier *Thomas P. Beal*, seen on sea trials in 1921. At the time, the collier was one of the largest ships ever built at the yard, second only to *Georgia*. Unfortunately, Bath could only get contracts for two large commercial ships—*Beal* and a sistership.

Thomas P. Beal's geared steam turbine engine is seen assembled in the Machine Shop. The condenser is at the left, the turbines at the center, and the reduction gear in the gearbox at the right. Although *Beal* was a large ship, it did not need to be fast, and this engine produced a scant 2,200 horsepower.

From 1922 to 1924, BIW built six lightships for the U.S. Light House Service. Here we see Light Vessel No. 91 launching on November 10, 1923. This lightship initially served on Pollock Rip Station. Nearly 80 years later, at least one of the 1920s Bath-built lightships, Light Vessel No. 107, still survives at a marina in New Jersey.

The last big Bath-built yacht in the postwar era was *Aras*, built for Hugh J. Chisholm, president of the Oxford Paper Company. The yard was falling on hard times but found work in building three small yachts and a series of 16 *Seawanhaka*-class schooners, each 58 feet in length. These were Bath's last yachts before bankruptcy in 1925. During these difficult times, Bath also diversified, building all manner of industrial items, from boilers to paper-making machinery.

The last major ship from Bath Iron Works was the coastal passenger steamer *Nobska*, built for the New England Steamship Company. Bath shut down operations in August 1925 and went into bankruptcy. The shipyard was sold at auction on October 1, 1925. One of the bidders was William "Pete" Newell, the yard's engineering and works manager, who hoped to reopen the shipyard. He was outbid, and the yard was sold, stripped of equipment, and lay idle.

Nobska had a long life, attesting to the quality of construction. After retiring from active service, the steamer spent years as a floating restaurant and more years laying idle and abandoned but is now being restored. In July 2001, *Nobska* was in Drydock No. 1 at the former Boston Navy Yard, undergoing extensive repair work while the original Bath-built steam engine was being restored elsewhere. The steamer was hoped to return to service along the New England coast. (Photograph by the author.)

Three

The Return of Shipbuilding: Bath Iron Works Reborn

Pete Newell persevered, even after he was unable to buy the defunct shipyard in 1925. Two years later, working with a small group of investors, he obtained a lease on the vacant shipyard property and purchased equipment from another defunct shipyard. Bath Iron Works Corporation was formed on October 1, 1927, bringing life back to the shipyard. Just a year later, the new Bath Iron Works' first ship, the yacht *Vanda*, prepares for launch on October 3, 1928. *Vanda* is flanked by the elevated craneways installed during the yard's World War I–era expansion, replacing the shiphouse and the old cable trolley system.

May 27, 1928, finds *Vanda* on the ways, the structure assembled up to the main deck just four months after construction started. This was the first of 19 yachts built by the yard prior to World War II. Nearly all 19 yachts went into military service as patrol craft when war broke out. *Vanda* became the Navy's *San Bernadino* and sailed the Pacific as a weather reporting ship.

The trawler was another mainstay of the reborn BIW, with 18 built before the war. Like the yachts, most joined the Navy in wartime, serving as minesweepers. The yard's bid for the first three trawlers was prepared in one day and night of frantic work. *Boston College*, launched 14 days after *Vanda*, was the result.

The 138-foot yacht *Paragon* is about to be launched from the Machine Shop on September 12, 1929. Like most yachts of this era, it is diesel powered, in contrast to the steam power common in Bath's earlier yachts. *Paragon* patrolled the Pacific coast from 1942 to 1944 but did not last long in naval service and was soon discarded. The cavernous size of the Machine Shop is evident in this view.

Paragon is taken in tow by the tug *Sequin* moments after launch. *Sequin* was the resident tug at Bath Iron Works and a common sight along the Kennebec for many years. The new Carlton Bridge looms in the background, carrying both the highway and the Maine Central Railroad across the Kennebec, rendering earlier ferries obsolete.

The big yacht *Hi-Esmaro*, built for H.E. Manville, goes down the ways in 1929 as employees and spectators move in for a better view. Eleven years later, the Navy took the yacht over as *Niagara*, using it first as a patrol ship and then as a support ship for small torpedo boats. Japanese aircraft crippled the ship on May 23, 1943, in the South Pacific. The squadron of PT boats rescued the crew and then torpedoed and sank *Niagara*.

As in the pre-bankruptcy years, Bath Iron Works obtained industrial contracts to supplement shipbuilding work. One customer was the Commonwealth Division of General Steel Casting Corporation, a builder of railroad equipment. Bath's Foundry cast many items for Commonwealth, including this locomotive tender component for South Australian Railways. For scale, note the man barely visible to the left.

Commercial sailing ships were largely a thing of the past by 1930, but sailing yachts were a different matter. The three-masted schooner yacht *Black Douglas* was launched on June 9, 1930, rigged and almost ready for delivery.

After a wartime stint with the Navy, *Black Douglas* went to the U.S. Fish and Wildlife Service as a research ship, seen in this *c.* 1949 view. By the late 1960s, the once proud yacht had become a floating power plant at a private island. Later, the yacht went through several restorations, eventually becoming a magnificent private yacht named *Aquarius*, offered for sale at $7 million in 2001—still rigged as a three-masted schooner. (Photograph courtesy NOAA.)

The Carlton Bridge's towers provide the vantage point for this 1929 photograph looking south over the shipyard. This is the yard's basic layout from the World War I–era expansion up to the start of the World War II era. In the right foreground is the abandoned Maine Central ferry slip. The shipyard is dominated by the big Machine Shop building, with ways extending from large doors in the east end. The Plate Shop is between the Machine Shop and the ways. The

J.P. Morgan's yacht *Corsair IV* was the largest private yacht built in the United States. The yacht was nearly complete when launched in April 1930 and is seen here six weeks later on trials off Rockland. Morgan was pleased and decided to take delivery immediately, sailing for New York after putting BIW's trial crew ashore at Rockland. The yacht went into the Royal Navy during the war and was wrecked on the Mexican coast in 1949.

Foundry, on the former Union Wharf property, lies between the Machine Shop and the ferry slip. The shipways have been expanded, with three raised craneways between them. At least five ships are being assembled on the ways—*Corsair IV* on the northern ways and four trawlers on the southern pair of ways. *Paragon* lies at the small pier between the ways. South of the yard's ways are the Houghton Shipyard and Hyde Windlass.

In contrast to *Corsair IV* is the diminutive *Dorothy*, a 36-foot workboat designed to tow log rafts on Rangeley Lake. The workboat was assembled in the Machine Shop in less than a month and is shown here nearly completed. *Dorothy* survived at least into the 1980s as a yacht.

Between 1929 and 1931, Bath built a series of five 190-foot stock yachts for H.J. Gielow Company (designers of many Bath-built yachts), which hoped to sell them to wealthy would-be yachtmen. The first of these, *Placida,* is on the ways on March 20, 1930, less than two months from launch.

Sylvia, the second stock yacht, is ready for launch on May 24, 1930. The owner is Logan G. Thompson, who has apparently brought his train right to the head of the ways. The stock yacht program was not a success. When the fifth yacht, *Aletes,* was being constructed, Gielow was insolvent and could neither pay for the yacht nor find a buyer, so Bath took possession and laid the yacht up in 1931. *Aletes* languished at the shipyard for a decade.

Another grand yacht of the 1930s was *Aras*, a replacement for the earlier Bath-built *Aras*. This 243-foot yacht traded a peacetime black hull for wartime gray in 1941 as USS *Williamsburg*. During the war, *Williamsburg* operated as a command-headquarters ship and transport. After the war, *Williamsburg* returned to its original purpose, becoming the presidential yacht for Pres. Harry S. Truman. Pres. Dwight D. Eisenhower ended the use of presidential yachts in 1953, and *Williamsburg* became a research ship until damaged in a drydocking accident in 1968. Thereafter, a series of plans to rehabilitate the ship fell apart, and by 1998, the old yacht was lying at Genoa, Italy, as a gutted hulk.

Two views aboard *Aras* show the grandeur of a 1930s yacht. The ship's cabins appear suitable for the finest mansion, and the meticulously finished decks are a perfect spot to enjoy the ocean. Sadly, all this fine craftsmanship was lost during transition to a warship. *Hi-Esmaro*, *Corsair IV*, *Aras* (II), and *Caroline* were Bath's biggest yachts of the postwar era, all well over 200 feet in length.

Seapine is nearly complete in the Machine Shop on April 17, 1931, less than two weeks away from launching. At 155 feet long and 496 tons displacement, *Seapine* was the largest vessel built indoors at Bath Iron Works. It appears the overhead crane, visible at the back of the shop, would barely clear the pilothouse. Renamed *Rhodolite,* the yacht sailed Hawaiian waters as a patrol ship and weather reporting vessel during the war. *Rhodolite* fared better than the yacht's original owner, Frank H. Goodyear, who perished before *Seapine* was completed.

The 550-horsepower, six-cylinder diesel engine aboard the trawler *Illinois* was delivered in 1931. The construction of trawlers continued in small groups right up to the World War II shipbuilding programs.

The last big yachts were *Felicia* and *Halonia*, a pair of similar 148-footers. *Felicia* differed in having a diesel-electric propulsion plant, the first Bath-built ship so equipped. The novelty of this feature accounts for this photograph of the switchboard panel. In naval service between 1942 and 1943, *Felicia* operated from Newport, Rhode Island, on anti-submarine patrols and then shifted to Boston as a training ship at Harvard.

A launching party is at BIW on November 9, 1931. The party is surely dry—Prohibition is in effect, and the ship being launched is the Coast Guard cutter *Thetis*, built to chase rumrunners. The state of the economy ended the era of big yachts, but a contract for the seven 165-foot cutters helped keep the yard afloat. *Thetis* was built in the Machine Shop, but the others were constructed on the ways outside.

The sixth of seven cutters, *Perseus* launches in April 1932. Like the other cutters, it was christened with Poland Spring Water instead of the traditional champagne. *Perseus*'s lines are graceful and yacht-like. All of the cutters served in the Navy during World War II, and all had long lives. *Calypso* and *Perseus* (Bath hulls No. 149 and No. 152, respectively) were sold out of service in the 1950s, but their stories did not end there.

The two cutters were acquired by the Circle Line of New York City and converted to passenger vessels named *Circle Line XI* and *Circle Line XV*. Both remain in service today. *Circle Line XV*, the former *Perseus*, is seen in spring 2002. On September 11, 2001, they were among the dozens of civilian vessels pressed into service in response to the terrorist attacks in that city. Each ship carried nearly 5,000 people across the river to New Jersey as lower Manhattan was evacuated. (William S. Bailey photograph.)

The cutters were powered by pairs of Winton 201A diesel engines. Each engine produced 670 horsepower, driving a 62-inch diameter propeller. The two cutters surviving as Circle Line ships still have their original Winton engines. After 70 years in service, the engines still operate reliably in daily service, carrying tourists around Manhattan.

With the Coast Guard cutters complete and the first destroyer contract not yet in hand, Bath went looking for fill-in work. One such job was the 61-foot boarding tug *T.B. McClintic* for the U.S. Public Health Service. The tug is seen in the shop with hull assembled up to the deck in August 1932. Profit on the contract was only $430. Later, the tug served as a fireboat for Wilmington, North Carolina.

The lighthouse tender *Hickory* was another fill-in job, returning a $220 profit. After installing diesel engines in all but one vessel built since the yard reopened in 1927, Bath built an old-fashioned reciprocating steam engine for *Hickory*. This engine, with polished linkages and cranks shining brightly, was the last engine of any type built by the shipyard. *Hickory* followed another group of lightships and was the yard's last job for the U.S. Light House Service.

The grandest and most famous ship of the late 1930s was *Ranger*, a 136-foot J-class racing sloop built to defend the America's Cup in the 1937 races. *Ranger*'s all-welded hull was built in the Machine Shop, as was the aluminum mast. With the mast secured on deck, the sloop was launched on May 11, 1937, reaching 18.5 knots coming down the ways. This was the last launching from the Machine Shop.

Ranger's crew poses on deck for a portrait.

Ranger's owner had the 165-foot mast stepped immediately after launch. Three days later, the sloop departed under tow to Newport, Rhode Island, for the races. Unfortunately, the mast and rigging were not suited to an ocean voyage in heavy seas. Part of the rigging failed, and the mast went overboard before *Ranger* could reach port. Bath immediately set to work on a new mast and worked around the clock until it was completed three weeks later.

Ranger is pictured under full sail. The sloop swept the cup races in 1937, the last of the great J-boats. Hauled out at the end of its first racing season, *Ranger* never floated again. Impending war in Europe made races in 1938 and 1939 impractical, and in 1941, *Ranger* was broken up for the war effort.

The double-ended Navy ferry *Aquidneck* of the late 1930s caused trouble for everyone. The rudder was damaged at launch—probably because there were rudders at bow and stern. While hauled out at South Portland for repairs, a fire broke out, causing damage and delays. On sea trials, *Aquidneck*'s electric motors overheated. By the time everything was set right, the ferry was nine months late and far overbudget.

Many of the 1930s contracts were taken for minimal profit, or even at a loss, to maintain the skilled workforce. Without the workforce, there would be no chance of getting more jobs, and BIW knew more destroyer jobs would be coming in due time. Here, Bath riveters work on a frame for a trawler, one of the fill-in jobs between destroyers. Within a few years, these men would be turning out destroyers at an astounding pace.

Four

Return of the Destroyers: Bath Iron Works Goes to War

In 1932, Bath Iron Works returned to the business of building destroyers for the Navy, laying the keel for *Dewey* (DD 349), which was launched on July 28, 1934. Fourteen years earlier, Bath had launched the Navy's last flush decker, *Pruitt* (DD 347). In the interim, the Navy built no destroyers. The drought was broken by *Dewey* and sistership *Farragut,* built at another shipyard. With these new ships, the Navy started rebuilding its destroyer fleet for the coming war, while also rebuilding the shipyards that would be needed for wartime construction.

Dewey's boilers were installed *c.* 1933. This unique A-frame crane was Bath's solution to lifting boilers, engines, and other equipment too heavy for conventional cranes, such as the one seen in the background. The A-frame and its supporting structure could be assembled over any of the shipways.

Dewey is on trials. The armament, not yet installed, included five 5-inch guns and eight torpedo tubes, in addition to light weapons. The modern destroyer's design is radically different from the old flush deckers, including a raised forecastle to keep the decks dry in heavy weather. During the Battle of the Coral Sea, *Dewey* went alongside the burning carrier *Lexington* to take off the crew, saving 112 men.

The Kennebec River was vital to the shipyard's existence, but sometimes caused problems. On March 23, 1936, the river ran high over its banks, putting much of the shipyard underwater. The second Bath destroyer of this era, *Drayton*, was supposed to be launched this day, but the flooding has forced a delay. *Drayton* was rated at 1,480 tons standard displacement, compared to 1,190 tons for the old flush deckers.

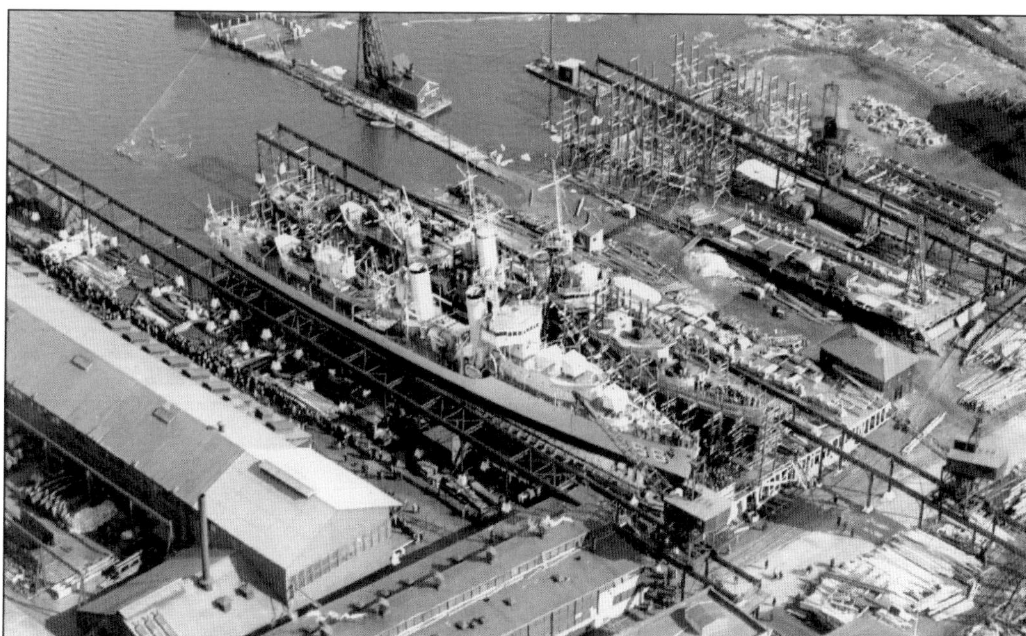

Just three days later, the river level is down, and although the yard is still littered with flood debris, *Drayton* will finally launch. The next destroyer, *Lamson*, is on the ways beside *Drayton*. This aerial view shows the center of the shipyard. The yard has expanded to the west, with craneways and buildings now extending to the west side of Water Street, which once formed the yard's western boundary.

Drayton hits 40 knots on sea trials in 1936. *Lamson* was faster still, reaching 41.43 knots. They were, and remain, the fastest destroyers ever built for the Navy. The twin destroyers were a slightly larger version of *Dewey*. Both fought during World War II in the Pacific and survived but were discarded in 1946—only 10 years old, but rendered obsolete by rapid changes in naval warfare.

Lamson's sponsor, Frances W. Andrews, is ready with her champagne bottle for the ceremonial christening on June 17, 1936. This was the third destroyer named in honor of Roswell Hawkes Lamson, a Civil War hero. The first was a contemporary of Bath's *Flusser*, and the second a short-lived flush decker decommissioned in 1930 when the boilers wore out.

Sampson was completed in 1938, representing a group of destroyer leaders. These bigger ships (1,850 tons nominal displacement) were supposed to bridge the gap between the small destroyers and big cruisers. They carried an impressive battery of eight 5-inch guns (two per turret) and 12 torpedo tubes, but the guns could only fire against ships, not aircraft, a major handicap in the coming war.

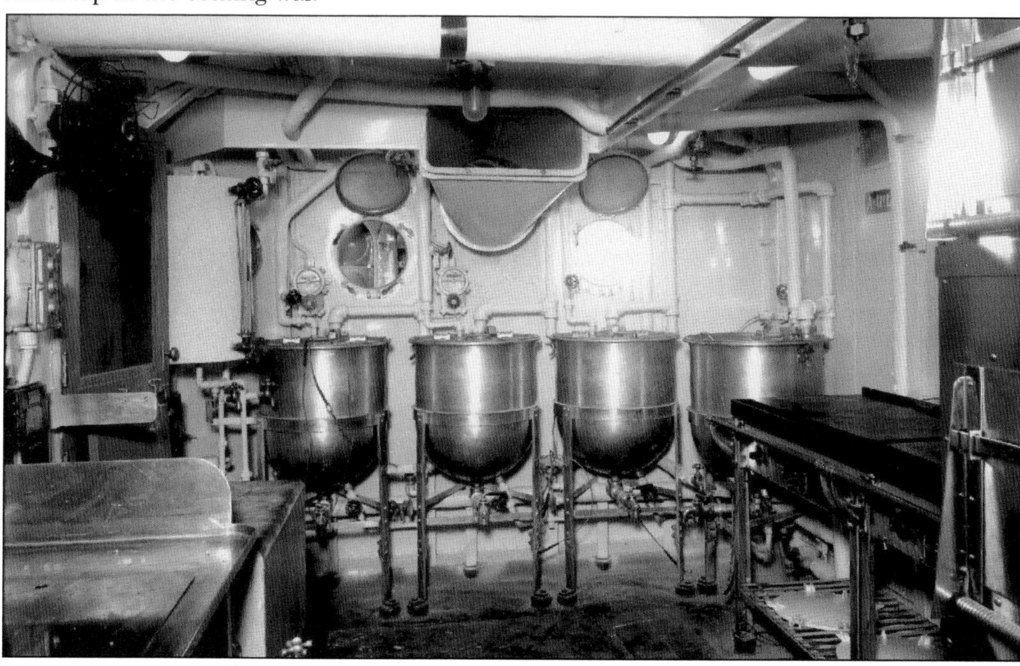

Sampson's spartan galley is in sharp contrast to the plush cabins aboard the yachts built earlier in the decade. The destroyers were purely functional and even lacked some amenities found aboard larger warships. This galley would feed the peacetime crew of about 200 men, and more in wartime.

Eberle is ready to slide in September 1940. The tide is high and men are under the ship, ready to drive the wedges in the launch cradle—the launching must be just minutes away. *Eberle* was one of the last prewar destroyers. Compared to the earlier leaders, it is a smaller ship, more suited for production in large numbers.

Jeanne D'Arc was the first of two 136-foot trawlers built for F.J. O'Hara & Sons of Rockland. They were Bath's last trawlers before the war, and the last for U.S. owners. The trawler contracts were signed to keep the yard busy until the wartime destroyer programs started.

While waiting for the wartime destroyer program, Bath landed its largest non-destroyer job—construction of four 420-foot fast freighters. The first, *Exceller,* lies outboard of the second, *Extavia,* in August 1941. Two destroyers are on the ways in the foreground. The small sailing yacht *Vagrant* is dwarfed by the warships and freighters around it.

Just six months earlier, on February 1, 1941, *Exceller* was unrecognizable as men work to clear snow and ice around the stern on the ways. Icy winter conditions such as these have always been a challenge for Bath's shipbuilders. The sternpost assembly, which will support the propeller and rudder, has just been erected.

This finely crafted model shows the finished appearance of the four freighters. Construction of such a model for each ship class is a longstanding tradition. These freighters carried military cargoes throughout the war but were not taken into naval service. One was damaged by enemy action, and another by a floating mine after the war ended.

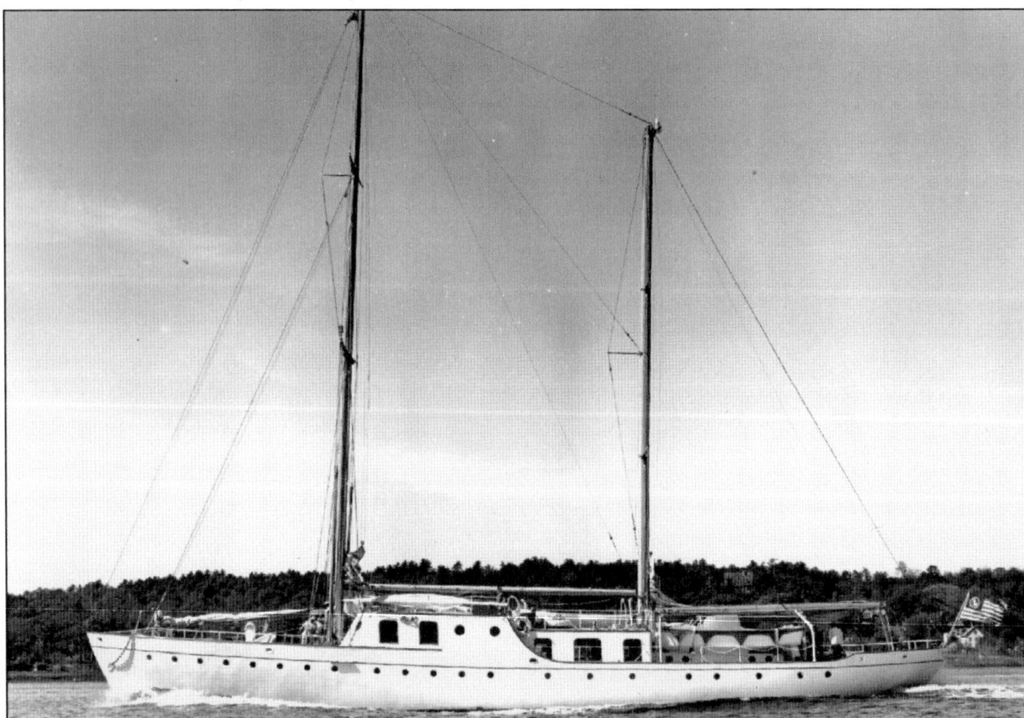

Harold Vanderbilt, owner of the J-boat *Ranger,* wanted the yacht *Vagrant* in 1940. Bath was busy with destroyers and freighters but accommodated an old friend's request. Critical materials were diverted to the war effort, and construction went slowly. *Vagrant* was delivered three months before Pearl Harbor and soon went into naval service as a patrol and training ship.

During World War II, Bath Iron Works functioned as a machine, turning out destroyers more quickly than previously thought possible—an average of one every 17 days. On August 16, 1942, *Conway* (left) and *Cony* were part of the "greatest mass launching in history." Eight ships were launched in Maine this day—this pair of destroyers, British freighters *Ocean Wayfarer*, *Ocean Stranger*, *Ocean Traveler*, *Ocean Seaman*, and *Ocean Gallant* at Todd-Bath Iron Shipbuilding, South Portland, and the Liberty Ship *Ethan Allen* from South Portland Shipbuilding. Within six months, *Conway* and *Cony* will be in combat in the Pacific. Both survived the war, served the Navy in peacetime, and were expended as target ships in 1969 and 1970. The two shipyards in South Portland were constructed for the wartime merchant shipbuilding programs and jointly operated by Bath Iron Works and Todd Shipbuilding. Later consolidated as New England Shipbuilding, the yards constructed 30 *Ocean*-class freighters for Great Britain and 244 Liberty Ships for United States merchant shipping and for the Navy.

The wartime destroyer programs started with *Fletcher*-class ships, which soon formed the backbone of the fleet. Bath built 31 *Fletchers*. The first were *Nicholas* and *O'Bannon*, seen here on April 1, 1941, one month after their keels were laid. *Aletes*, left over from the 1930s stock yacht program, remains at the pier in the background. In a month, the yacht will be sold to the Navy and immediately transferred to the Royal Navy for service as an escort ship.

Nine months later, on January 1, 1942, the new destroyers are well along, nearing launch. These ships were built in the conventional way—piece by piece on the shipways, with little preassembly. They were 11½ months from keel laying to launch, with another 4 months to delivery, consuming about 1,354,000 man-hours of labor. These figures would all be significantly reduced before the war ended.

Launch day for *Nicholas* was February 19, 1942. *O'Bannon*, to the right, will launch one month later. The *Fletchers* were big ships—2,100-ton standard displacement (bigger than the leaders of the 1930s), carrying five 5-inch guns and 10 torpedoes, plus a heavy anti-aircraft gun battery. A 60,000-horsepower steam turbine plant gave them a speed of about 36 knots.

Nicholas was on sea trials in May 1942. Although numerically the fifth ship of its class, *Nicholas* was the first completed and therefore ran a full set of sea trials. Subsequent ships of the class skipped sea trials and sailed directly from Bath to Boston Navy Yard for delivery, cranking up to full speed immediately after clearing the Kennebec.

Bath Iron Works undertook a major expansion in 1940 and 1941, including the purchase of the Maine Central Railroad yard and former ferry slip at the north end of the shipyard. The space was used to build a new set of shipways, a warehouse, and an assembly building; the north pier was also rebuilt. On July 1, 1941, the new north ways are incomplete and the cranes are not yet assembled, but construction of the destroyers *Strong* and *Chevalier* has already begun.

In a scene repeated 86 times between 1940 and 1945, a destroyer slides down the ways. Launchings were on Sundays to minimize disruption to other work in the shipyard. Bath built one fourth of the Navy's destroyers during this period, more destroyers than all of Japan's shipyards produced in the same time.

Exactly one year after the first view of *Chevalier* and *Strong*, the two ships lie together at the north pier (left). To the right, *Taylor* and *De Haven* are moored at the end of the north ways. These are Bath's second and third pair of *Fletchers*, following *Nicholas* and *O'Bannon*. The wartime careers of these ships were strangely linked. A year after this photograph, early in the morning of July 5, 1943, *Nicholas* and *Strong* shelled Bairoko Harbor, New Guinea. *Strong* was mortally wounded by Japanese torpedoes, and *Chevalier* came to the ship's aid, intentionally ramming the doomed destroyer so the crew could scramble to safety. *Chevalier* took off 241 men in seven minutes as *O'Bannon* lay down covering fire against Japanese shore batteries. Three months later, on October 6, *Chevalier*'s luck ran out. One of three destroyers attacking a force of nine Japanese destroyers in the Solomons, *Chevalier* was torpedoed. The ship ran out of control, and *O'Bannon* was unable to avoid a collision. The torpedo and collision doomed *Chevalier*, and *O'Bannon* rescued the crew.

Skilled personnel were key to the war effort, and Bath went to great lengths to hire and retain a workforce of about 12,000 men and women during the war. This photograph shows a group of "champion riveters," probably aboard *Cony*, on May 7, 1942. Productivity contests were common as a means to inspire quicker work.

Mrs. William R. Slight christens *Cony* on August 16, 1942, the day of the "greatest mass launching." The role of sponsor, although ceremonial, is important to the ship's identity and history.

A huge crowd has gathered around the north ways for the launch of *Spence* on Navy Day, October 27, 1942. The new North Stores warehouse and the North Yard Assembly Building are to the right. The north ways are built up on wooden pilings because steel and concrete were in limited supply during the war. Sadly, just over two years later, *Spence* was sunk in a typhoon with only 24 survivors.

Abbott was launched on February 17, 1943, in a snowstorm. In peacetime, bad weather might have delayed the launch, but in wartime there could be no delay. Unless weather conditions made a launch unsafe, it would go ahead even if the spectators were frozen.

Part of the wartime expansion was the purchase of the old Houghton shipyard at the yard's south end. This new Boiler Shop was built on the site, removing boiler assembly work from the Machine Shop. Here, a group of boilers, the standard type in wartime destroyers, is undergoing final assembly. With four boilers per ship, more than 300 of these boilers were installed at Bath during the wartime programs.

One end of the Boiler Shop was used for final check-out and polishing of propellers. A group of machinists is seen buffing propeller blades, getting them ready for shipboard installation on the ways.

These destroyers are stacked four deep at the north pier—*Knapp*, *Ingersoll*, *Caperton* and *Cogswell*. Putting ships three- or four-abreast did cause problems, including inability of the pierside cranes to reach the outer ships. A mechanic working on the outboard ship would regret forgetting a tool on the pier, after hiking across four ships.

Barton was Bath's first of a new destroyer type, the *Allen M. Sumner*-class 2,200-tonners. Bath built 20 of these ships, slightly enlarged versions of the earlier *Fletchers*, boasting six 5-inch guns, two per turret. In most other respects, they were the same, so they could be built without delay. As with the *Fletcher* class, Bath completed its first ship before the numerical first of the class was finished at another yard. Thus, *Barton* runs sea trials on the Rockland measured mile, coated in ice, in December 1943.

Tolman represents a slight variation on the *Sumners*. As destroyer-minelayers, some ships sacrificed torpedo tubes in favor of rails to carry and launch naval mines. The rails are barely visible near the stern as the camouflaged ship cuts through sea spray.

The Bath-built destroyer *O'Brien* saw plenty of action, being damaged in action on the French coast and twice in the Pacific. *O'Brien* rescued the crew of the stricken transport *Ward* and here assists other destroyers alongside the burning landing ship LST 472, fighting fires and taking off 198 of the crew.

Getting employees from their homes to BIW was a major challenge, as the roads and vehicles simply were not adequate. Bath's solution was a massive fleet of customized buses, running from this former car dealership in downtown Bath. Employees of Department 29, the transportation department, pose in front of the building.

The pipe shop, Department 15, displays its "gadgets" during a productivity-improvement event. All these bits of hardware were intended to speed up production in the name of efficiency and patriotism.

This is *Frank Knox*, just after launch on September 17, 1944. *Frank Knox* was Bath's first 2,250-ton *Gearing*-class destroyer, a variant of the *Sumner*-class design with a 14-foot section added amidships, between the funnels. By war's end, these ships required 677,262 man-hours of labor, going from keel laying to launch in four months, with delivery just three months later—a remarkable improvement from the prewar statistics.

Keeping up the tradition, the yard finished *Frank Knox* before the official class lead ship. During sea trials, seen here, the ship exceeded 36 knots on the Rockland trials range. The *Gearing*-class formed the backbone of the Navy's postwar destroyer fleet, and many served well into the 1990s in foreign navies. *Knox* lasted until 1992 in the Greek navy.

This is a view of the yard's center and south end at the end of the war, summer 1945. The six shipways are now served by five elevated craneways, and a new south pier has been constructed for post-launch outfitting. The new Boiler Shop is immediately beyond the ways; the Hyde Windlass plant lies farther south. Six destroyers on the ways are in varying stages of completion, ranging from early assembly to nearly ready for launch.

This is the corresponding view of the yard's north end. There are two destroyers on the north ways, bordering the remaining railroad yard. The new buildings are the North Stores warehouse and the North Yard Assembly Building, nearest to the expanded north pier, all built on the former railroad ferry terminal property. The older buildings—the Plate Shop, Machine Shop, and Foundry—are largely unchanged.

War's end left two ships unfinished at Bath. Construction of *Robert A. Owens* was suspended by the Navy in January 1946, when the ship was 70 percent complete—only the funnels stood above the deck. *Owens* was launched and delivered to the Navy, incomplete, the following July, going into storage for potential future use. Four other destroyers were cancelled before construction began.

Timmerman was only 45 percent complete when the suspension order came through. This view in the aft engine room shows the bare steel structure of the ship, with light streaming through the unfinished deck overhead. *Timmerman* would remain on the ways well into the postwar years and was eventually completed to a modified design.

Five

POSTWAR TRANSITION: TRAWLERS AND DESTROYERS

The postwar years at Bath Iron Works were a transitional time, both for the shipyard and for the ships. While some ships represented World War II–era ideas and technology, others focused on new innovations. *Mitscher* was a hybrid—conceived during the war as the ultimate destroyer, but delivered in 1953 with a host of new weapons and systems, many of them largely experimental. In the course of construction, *Mitscher* was reclassified from destroyer (DD 927) to frigate (DL 2) because the ship was so much larger than previous destroyers.

This view of the shipyard in early 1947 finds three Navy cargo ships alongside being converted to commercial freighters. A fourth such vessel was converted to a schoolship for the Maine and Massachusetts Maritime Academies. At the far end of the yard, two incomplete destroyers lie alongside the Hyde Windlass plant. The empty property beyond them is the recently burned-down Bath Box Company.

The end of yacht construction at Bath came in 1947. The yard's only postwar yacht, the 167-foot *Haida*, was launched on May 3, 1947, and delivered three months later. From 1947 to 1949, Bath also rebuilt a former Navy gunboat as the yacht *Elpetal*, reversing the Navy's wartime conversion. *Elpetal* survived at least into the 1980s, and *Haida* still operates today, named *Astarte*.

The biggest postwar job—and the yard's largest-ever contract, in terms of number of hulls—was the construction of 32 trawlers for the French government, to replace the fishing fleet destroyed in wartime. There were twenty 117-foot vessels, six 152-footers, and six 240-footers, such as *Heureux*. The project was not without problems, however, including delayed delivery of steel at inflated prices. The 240-footers were the largest trawlers yet built in the country.

Another problem was instability of the 152-foot trawlers, due to insufficient ballast and excessive superstructure. Bath's recommendations to correct the situation were only partially accepted by the owners. *Clair De Lune* demonstrates the problem on launch day, taking a dramatic list as the crew rushes to the rail, while those ashore look on in shock. Fortunately, the trawler stabilized at this point and was safely brought to the pier without further incident. The yard had a few embarrassing launch incidents over the years, but never a disaster.

The manufacturers of diesel engines and winches also had problems, including late delivery and poor performance. The result was a massive backlog of trawlers at the yard's piers and elsewhere in Bath as the yard waited to receive equipment and tried to resolve the problems. When all was set right, the trawlers sailed for France, carrying donated flour and other relief supplies for the war-ravaged country.

The trawler program brought triple launchings to BIW for the first time. *Saint Joachim*, *Doux Frimaire*, and *Patron Roger Dupuy* were all launched on October 30, 1948. They were the final ships in the program and the third three-in-one-day launch. A few of the trawlers are still in service today, a testament to the quality of the yard's workmanship in spite of the challenges of the job.

The first postwar destroyer contract was for the completion and conversion of two never-completed *Gearing*-class destroyers. *Epperson* (left) and *Robert A. Owens* (right), seen in January 1948, were to become prototypes for two types of postwar destroyers. *Owens* was Bath-built, delivered incomplete in 1946 after construction was cancelled. The stalwart old tug *Sequin* is moored alongside the craneway in this view.

Epperson was built at another shipyard, so Bath carefully documented its as-received condition, photographing every space aboard ship. This view of the forward boiler room shows two of the four boilers and some of the tangled piping common in machinery spaces. Both destroyer conversions retained the original propulsion plants but received new weapons and new aluminum superstructures.

Robert A. Owens was completed in 1949 as a hunter-killer destroyer (DDK 827), intended to destroy modern fast submarines. The armament originally planned for *Gearing*-class ships was eliminated in favor of modern anti-submarine rockets and anti-aircraft guns for self-defense. Compare this view to the *Gearing*-class ships on pages 70 and 71. *Epperson*, completed as an escort destroyer (DDE 719), retained more original armament to suit a convoy escort role.

Timmerman, left incomplete on the ways when the war ended, was another experimental *Gearing*-class conversion. Modifications emphasized improved propulsion machinery rather than new weapons. *Timmerman* received an experimental high-pressure steam propulsion plant, producing 100,000 horsepower instead of 60,000 in its conventional sisters. The destroyer also had an advanced, lightweight electrical plant and an all-aluminum superstructure. The superstructure was placed aboard in a rare three-crane lift on November 16, 1950.

The experimental propulsion plant was also incorporated into *Mitscher* and *John S. McCain*, even before *Timmerman* had tried out the equipment. This was unfortunate because the new boilers, operating at 1,200-pounds-per-square-inch pressure, turned out to be complex and delicate beasts. One of *Mitscher*'s boilers has a radically different appearance compared to the conventional 600-pounds-per-square-inch boilers seen on page 66.

Timmerman sits alongside *Mitscher* at the north pier. *Gearing*-class ships such as *Timmerman* were considered huge destroyers during World War II, but *Mitscher* is 100 feet longer and 50 percent heavier. *Timmerman* remained at the yard for fine-tuning into 1952 and was decommissioned after only a few years of experimental service. *Mitscher* was completed a year later and had a long life, lasting until 1978, following a modernization and conversion to install guided missiles.

The second big frigate was *John S. McCain*, launched from the north ways on July 12, 1952. The ships' size required reconstruction of the ways to accommodate them—the north ways received a new concrete extension for *McCain*'s construction. Ironically, this was the last ship built on the north ways, and the concrete ways extension seen under *McCain*'s bow was later converted into a garage for the maintenance department.

In contrast to the frigates was Bath's smallest-ever naval vessel, the 89-foot experimental patrol boat PT 810. Constructed in the North Yard Assembly Building, as seen in this February 16, 1949 view, it was the last vessel built indoors at BIW. PT 810 was also Bath's fastest ship, exceeding 47 knots on trials. Although the patrol boat was small, construction took two years.

PT 810 was carefully winched down the ways in a specially built cradle on June 2, 1950. The torpedo boats of the 1890s, such as *T.A.M. Craven*, had been launched by a similar method to protect their delicate hulls. The experimental vessels of 1947 to 1953—*Owens*, *Epperson*, *Timmerman*, *Mitscher*, *McCain*, and PT 810, put Bath at the forefront of warship technology and in good position to build the Navy's newest ships.

The next Navy contract was quite a change—five slow landing ships featuring no revolutionary technology. Although lacking the glamour of fast destroyers, they were good work and kept the yard busy. *Terrebone Parish* (LST 1156), the first of the class, is shown on Popham Beach at the mouth of the Kennebec, demonstrating its ability to land heavy vehicles directly onto the shore.

On July 1, 1953, the shipyard is busy again. A landing ship, *Tom Green County*, is on the ways to the left, ready to launch the next day. Another LST is at the pier in the right background. At the center is *Dealey* (DE 1006), the first of three destroyer escorts built between 1952 and 1955. The DEs were simple ships, essentially a smaller, slower version of a destroyer, meant to be built rapidly in wartime.

Hammerberg, third of the destroyer escorts, is on sea trials in 1955. To keep the ships simple, they carried 3-inch, 50-caliber anti-aircraft gun mounts forward and aft, and a Weapon Able anti-submarine rocket launcher just forward of the bridge. In contrast, the big *Mitscher* carried the same 3-inch guns, two Weapon Ables, and two rapid-fire 5-inch, 54-caliber guns. *Hammerberg* achieved 27.5 knots; *Mitscher* did 36.5 knots.

The 1950s saw some investment in the shipyard's facilities and replacement of equipment and machinery worn out during the war. The old blacksmith shop is seen here in October 1956 after a complete rebuilding and conversion to a sheetmetal shop. New cranes in the background have replaced older cranes, some of which had dated to the World War I–era shipyard modernization.

This view looks inside the newly rebuilt sheetmetal shop, always known as the tin shop. The tinsmiths are fabricating some ducts—perhaps for a ship, perhaps for some of the non-shipboard industrial products manufactured in the postwar years. Slow and sporadic shipbuilding contracts caused Bath to pursue a wide variety of industrial work.

The Machine Shop in April 1954 shows a dramatic transformation from earlier views. The days of indoor shipbuilding here are over, and the shop floor is filled with machines—some new in the postwar years, and some much older. A coat of white paint has considerably improved the atmosphere as well. Also in the 1950s, the old wooden north pier, continually expanded over the years, was completely rebuilt in concrete.

The east end of the old Plate Shop, built to house the 1899 torpedo boats, was demolished in 1953 to make way for a new electric shop. The new shop can be seen above the bow of *Somers* on page 86. The remainder of the old Plate Shop later served as a sheetmetal shop and was gradually demolished over the years, replaced by new shop buildings.

The biggest addition to the shipyard was construction of the new Structural Assembly Building across the west end of the ways. Completed in 1956, the 514-foot-long building was part of a fundamental change in the way ships were built. Switching from piece-built to modular or unit construction, large sections of the ship were fabricated and assembled in the shop, then taken to the ways for final integration into the ship.

A hull section comes out of the new Assembly Building and heads to the ways, carried by two cranes. The craneways have been extended right up to the building, and the area between the ways and the building serves as storage for ship components and equipment. This unit construction approach offered enormous efficiencies compared to traditional methods. In this era, the yard could handle assemblies up to 50 tons in weight.

A welder puts final touches on an aluminum smokestack for the destroyer *Forrest Sherman* c. 1954. The stack is lying down alongside one of the yard's craneways. *Forrest Sherman* and its sisters were a middle ground between big frigates such as *Mitscher* and small escorts such as *Dealey*. Not intended to fight submarines, they were armed with three 5-inch guns and two twin 3-inch anti-aircraft gun mounts.

Forrest Sherman–class destroyers *Hull, Edson, and Somers*, shown from left to right, are in varying stages of completion. The yard built nine of these ships, fully half of the class. They were the last Bath ships with guns as their primary armament, as the guided missile era was rapidly approaching. *Edson* survives today as a museum in New York City, and the Bath-built *Barry* is preserved in the nation's capital.

Shipbuilding is a business of details, such as machining the strut to receive propeller shaft bearings. The boring operation is carried out with this complex machine seen under *Somers* on the ways *c.* 1957. The machining ensures the strut, which supports the propeller shaft and the propeller itself, is properly aligned. Careful work by skilled machinists at this stage will help keep the propulsion plant in good working order for many years.

The Bath Iron Works trial crew is on the bridge of *Somers* during sea trials on February 17, 1959. The ships are owned and operated by BIW until delivered to the customer after trials. Capt. Charles W. Spear (center) is responsible for safe operation of the ship throughout sea trials. *Somers* was rebuilt with guided missiles in 1967 and was in service until 1982; it was sunk as a target ship in 1998.

An aerial view of the shipyard in 1957 shows the facility's evolution since World War II. The destroyers *Du Pont* and *Bigelow* are at the north pier; *Hull, Edson*, and *Somers* are on the ways. The yard is reduced from eight ways during the war to four ways now, as larger ships have forced wider and longer ways. The north ways, to the left, are now abandoned, but their cranes remain in place. The new Structural Assembly Building has pushed the yard's borders farther west to Washington Street. To the Assembly Building's right is the new main office building, constructed in 1940 and also bordering on Washington Street. The yard's other major buildings are little changed from the 1945 photographs on page 71, aside from the new electric shop just above the pierside destroyers.

Six

The Guided Missile Era and Commercial Shipbuilding

The 1960s brought two distinct shipbuilding programs to Bath Iron Works—the Navy's guided missile warships and commercial ships. The guided missile frigate *Leahy* (DLG 16), launched on July 1, 1961, combined new propulsion machinery and aluminum superstructures, pioneered in the yard's postwar experimental ships, and guided missile technology tested in rebuilt war-era vessels. The result was the Navy's first all-new-design first-line guided missile warship, one of eight similar ships built at Bath.

Bath's first guided missile ships were the frigates *Dewey* (DLG 14) and *Preble* (DLG 15), seen at the pier on July 6, 1953. They were transitional ships, as their basic design was similar to the earlier *Mitscher* with a missile launcher added aft. They were originally intended to carry two 5-inch guns forward, but an eight-cell launcher for the new ASROC anti-submarine rocket was substituted just forward of the bridge (not yet installed in these views).

Dewey's missile launcher is aimed toward the camera, with dummy missiles on the rails. The *Terrier* missiles were stowed in a below-decks magazine and slid out through the doors left of the launcher. *Dewey* and *Preble* were the last ships of a 10-unit class, but Bath delivered both before other yards completed a single ship.

The pioneer guided missile frigates (DLGs) were followed by four guided missile destroyers, starting with *Charles F. Adams* (DDG 2), seen on the ways on April 1, 1959. *Preble* is in the background, about two months from launch. The *Adams*-class ships were enlarged versions of Bath's earlier *Forrest Sherman* class, with a 40-round missile launcher aft. These ships were smaller than the DLGs and carried the shorter-ranged *Tartar* missile.

Nearly four decades later, in March 1998, *Adams* is seen in the mothball fleet at Philadelphia, awaiting its fate with other decommissioned ships. *Adams* served the Navy for 30 years, and there is hope the ship may become a museum, preserving one of a class that once numbered 29 ships in U.S. and foreign service. (Craig Pulver photograph.)

A welder works inside a lower hull unit for *Worden*, the second guided missile frigate, in the Structural Assembly Building. Work in the building was much easier and more efficient than work outside in the weather.

Leahy is on trials. The ship's profile is futuristic, with combined masts and smokestacks known as macks, supporting big air-search radars. Smaller missile guidance radars are mounted on the superstructure forward and aft. Many guided missile frigates came to Bath for major overhauls in the late 1960s and early 1970s, although *Leahy* was not among them. In 1975, they were all reclassified as guided missile cruisers (CGs), as the Navy reorganized its ship designation system. They served into the 1990s.

Keel laying for *Belknap* was on February 5, 1962. With unit-system construction, the "keel" is actually a chunk of the hull structure, rather than a single beam, as was common in traditional shipbuilding methods. *Belknap* was Bath's fourth guided missile frigate and the first of a modified design, which eliminated one missile launcher in favor of a 5-inch gun and a flight deck and hangar for small helicopters.

Belknap (DLG 26) and *Josephus Daniels* fitting out on a frigid January 2, 1964. *Belknap* is best remembered for a horrific collision with the aircraft carrier *John F. Kennedy* in which *Belknap*'s aluminum superstructure burned and melted, with disastrous results. This led to the Navy's later decision to return to all-steel superstructures in the interests of safety and durability. *Belknap* was repaired and later served as flagship of the U.S. Sixth Fleet.

William H. Standley (DLG 32) is on the ways on October 5, 1964. The white structure to the right is the yard's bow dock, a pseudo-drydock designed to provide access for underwater work on the ships' sonar domes. The dock appears ready for launch, which turned into quite an event, as the dock got sideways and stuck in the mud while sliding down the ways. It was later hauled off by a fleet of tugs.

Biddle (DLG 34), Bath's last guided missile frigate, and *Julius A. Furer* (DEG 6) are fitting out. *Furer*'s bow is in the bow dock during installation of the bulbous dome housing the ship's sonar system. Because the dome projects far below the keel, it could not be installed before the ship was launched. *Furer* is one of three guided missile destroyer escorts built at Bath, the descendants of the 1950s *Dealy*-class ships.

Glover was generally similar to *Julius A. Furer* and other contemporary escort ships (DEs or DEGs) but was built as an experimental ship. The biggest experiment was a Bath-designed pumpjet instead of a traditional propeller. *Glover* spent its career in a variety of roles, testing propulsion systems, sonars, and other systems, and briefly serving as an operational warship. This was the last major warship built by the Navy for purely experimental and testing purposes.

Bath's final guided missile ships of this era were a trio of modified *Adams*-class guided missile destroyers (DDGs) built for the German navy. *Rommel* is coming down the ways on February 1, 1969, while its sisters *Lutjens* and *Molders* are at the pier. Although their sisters in the U.S. Navy and Australian navy have been retired, two German ships (and a few former U.S. ships in the Greek navy) remain in service.

Bath Iron Works was a finalist in the 1960s competition to design and build the DX-class destroyer, a general-purpose ship meant to replace the aging fleet of World War II–era destroyers. This model shows the layout of Bath's design, prepared for BIW by Gibbs & Cox. Unfortunately for Bath, the Navy chose the competitor's design. It was a winner-take-all competition, so Bath received none of the DX program work.

Accompanying the DX-class proposal was this proposal for a massively expanded and rebuilt shipyard. The centerpiece was a huge land-level ship assembly area, stretching downriver from the existing shipyard and consuming the Hyde Windlass property. Ships would be built on a flat platform and then transferred sideways onto a drydock for launching. The proposal was abandoned when Bath lost the DX program.

Even before the DX loss, and more so afterwards, Bath looked toward commercial shipbuilding. The first ship in the commercial program, the 610-foot container ship *Sea Witch*, towers over a German destroyer on the ways. Nine ships of this design were built over several years. The success of the commercial shipbuilding program lead to an even more ambitious, but never realized, shipyard growth plan based on the DX-era expansion plan.

Sea Witch clears the Kennebec River. At 7,100 tons light ship displacement and 26,670 tons full load, these ships finally surpassed Bath's old size record set by the battleship *Georgia* in 1906. *Sea Witch* was later involved in a spectacular collision and fire from which only the stern section was salvaged and rebuilt into a new ship. Today, three of *Sea Witch*'s sisterships are in the Navy's reserve fleet, refitted as crane ships.

An aerial view of the shipyard shows the next round of improvements under way. A new Assembly Building, to the south of the 1956 building, provides a larger facility for assembly of ship units. While container ship construction goes forward, the third shipway is being demolished and rebuilt as a craneway for a new, much larger crane, giving the yard the capability to handle ship components up to 220 tons.

The new No. 11 crane towers over the shipways in this east-looking view. The ways have been rebuilt, with concrete and steel replacing the old wooden structures. The huge 220-ton capacity crane has rendered the old cranes obsolete, and most of the craneways have been demolished. There are now three shipways—A and B north (left) of the crane, and C to the south.

The merchant shipbuilding program included seven commercially owned tankers built for long-term charter to the Navy. Five were 587-foot *Sealift*-class tankers such as *Sealift Caribbean*, and two were 688-foot *Falcon*-class ships. The *Falcons* were Bath's last commercial ships. When their charters expired, the *Sealift*- and *Falcon*-class ships entered merchant service, where most remain today.

Probably the most unusual Bath-built ship in recent times was this electric power generation barge built for General Electric. Named *Electron*, it was delivered in 1973 and towed to South America to generate power in remote areas lacking normal electric utilities.

Maine was the first of four big roll-on/roll-off vehicle cargo ships built at Bath. *Maine*'s May 24, 1975 launch will long be remembered. At 14,000 tons launch weight, the big ship did nearly 15 miles per hour going down the ways, and nine tugs struggled to control the ship in the river. When finally brought under control, the ship was perilously close to the Carlton Bridge and the east bank of the river.

Maine's problems were not over yet. Its sister *Arizona* ran out of control when launched a few months later, once again endangering the bridge. As tugs strained to hold *Arizona*, the wave created by the launch snapped *Maine*'s mooring lines, and the wind pushed the ship away from the pier. In this view, as a few safety lines hold the ship, the shipyard crew rushes to get the situation under control.

The massive No. 11 crane meant huge sections of ships could be preassembled and outfitted with equipment and then installed. The superstructure of the container ship *Maui* demonstrates this approach, as the 400-foot-tall crane gently places the enormous structure aboard the ship in a single lift. *Maui* was the largest ship ever built at Bath, and the largest built north of Boston.

The 720-foot *Maui* is lit by the crane's floodlights shortly before launch. This launch was another troubled one, as part of the cradle collapsed, smashing the ship's bow against the concrete ways and creating a "boom" heard and remembered throughout the shipyard. *Maui* was a very successful ship in the West Coast–Hawaii trade.

Toward the end of the merchant shipbuilding program, there were some unusual jobs, including the huge sugar barge HSTC-1, built for the California & Hawaii Sugar Company. The 634-foot barge was the largest yet built in the country. As tugs corral the just-launched barge, the wooden launch cradle floats off the end of the ways, successfully pulled from beneath the ship as it completed the launch run.

Another oddity was the dredge *Essayons*, built for the Army Corps of Engineers—the first and last time Bath had built a vessel for the U.S. Army. The work was actually done under subcontract from another shipyard, which was in bankruptcy and could not build the ship itself. *Essayons* was built beside the sugar barge, and part of the dredge's superstructure is seen in the foreground of the previous photograph.

As the commercial program started to wind down, Bath found new Navy work—the *Oliver Hazard Perry* (FFG 7) class guided missile frigates. These smaller, simpler ships were successors to the destroyer escorts (DEs and DEGs) of the 1950s and 1960s (the Navy's ship designation system had been completely overhauled in the interim). *Perry*'s keel was laid with the massive bulk of *Arizona* looming in the background.

The FFG program brought some interesting events, such as the delivery of reduction gears by air. The gears were purchased by the government and supplied to the shipyard, and it was apparently more efficient to transport them from the California factory by Air Force C-5A *Galaxy* airlifter instead of by truck. After unloading at nearby Naval Air Station Brunswick, they were trucked to Bath for installation.

Oliver Hazard Perry's launch was a most memorable event, as one of the guests was actor John Wayne. At the moment of christening, the ship refused to slide, so the actor leaned on the bow and appeared to push (left). At the same time hydraulic rams, installed for just this purpose, were used to "start" the ship, and *Perry* slid into the Kennebec while the actor posed for photographs with the ship in the background.

Perry on sea trials demonstrates the modern design of the class. A 40-round missile launcher is forward, and a 3-inch gun is atop the superstructure. Aft there is a flight deck and hangar for two helicopters, used to track submarines. The ships feature gas turbine propulsion, using two aircraft-type jet engines instead of steam turbines or diesels.

The number of guided missile frigates to be built, and growing overhaul business, forced the shipyard to acquire a drydock. This pre–World War I relic, a five-section dock of wooden construction, was purchased for a bargain-basement price. The dock allowed Bath to lift smaller ships in-house, rather than sending them to other shipyards for underwater work. *Perry* was the first ship to use the "new" dock.

Perhaps not surprisingly, the ancient dock had problems. The planking of one side wall failed while lifting a second ship, the frigate *Brumby*, causing the dock to take an alarming list. As a result, Bath constructed new steel wingwalls to mate with the existing wooden pontoon deck, strengthening the entire structure. In this view, the old walls are being demolished in preparation for the installation of their replacements. With the new walls in place, the drydock remained serviceable for many more years, until newer facilities were available.

With a 24 ships built at Bath Iron Works, the guided missile frigate program somewhat resembled the wartime destroyer programs, and ships were stacked deeply at the piers. The ships are, from left to right, *Gallery*, *Stephen W. Groves*, *Clifton Sprague*, *Estocin*, and *John L. Hall*, which has just been launched. *Aubrey Fitch* is on the ways in the left background. Many FFGs were built two-abreast on the C-ways.

The yard is at the peak of the FFG program. To the left, the Assembly Building has been doubled in length into the former Hyde Windlass property, whose buildings fill the space between the "AB" and the river. The drydock, alongside the new finger pier, has lifted a guided missile destroyer for overhaul. There are four FFGs at the south pier, and an older frigate is being overhauled at the north pier.

Seven

Portland and Hardings: Bath's Off-Site Facilities

The Portland Ship Repair Facility was Bath's largest off-site facility. Portland served dual purposes, carrying out overhauls on older vessels and doing underwater work on Bath's new-construction ships. Here, the Portland yard is seen at its peak, with the destroyer *Arleigh Burke* lifted in the big new drydock, the cruiser *Shiloh* at the long pier in the background, and two Coast Guard cutters undergoing overhaul at the other pier. The old wooden drydock from Bath has been moved to Portland and is moored just ahead of the Coast Guard vessels.

Bath's first off-site facility was the Hardings steel fabrication plant, constructed in 1940 in East Brunswick, about three miles from the main shipyard. The plant was constructed in haste during the prewar expansion program—ground was broken in July 1940, and the plant was operating by December. The Navy paid for construction, and the building was already 70 percent complete when a Navy official arrived to inspect the proposed site and blueprints.

The warehouse building at Hardings nears completion in January 1941. The plant included a steel fabrication building, steel storage yards, a warehouse, and a galvanizing facility. All steel receipt, storage, preparation, and cutting operations and fabrication of small structural assemblies were eventually moved to Hardings. This freed space in the crowded shipyard and allowed conversion of the old Plate Shop for other purposes.

The main fabrication bay of the Hardings plant, seen in 1954, is full of steel in various stages of cutting, bending, and assembly. The main building was 750 feet long and 90 feet wide, and the second floor housed a mold loft of equal dimensions, for lofting (drawing) ship components full-size.

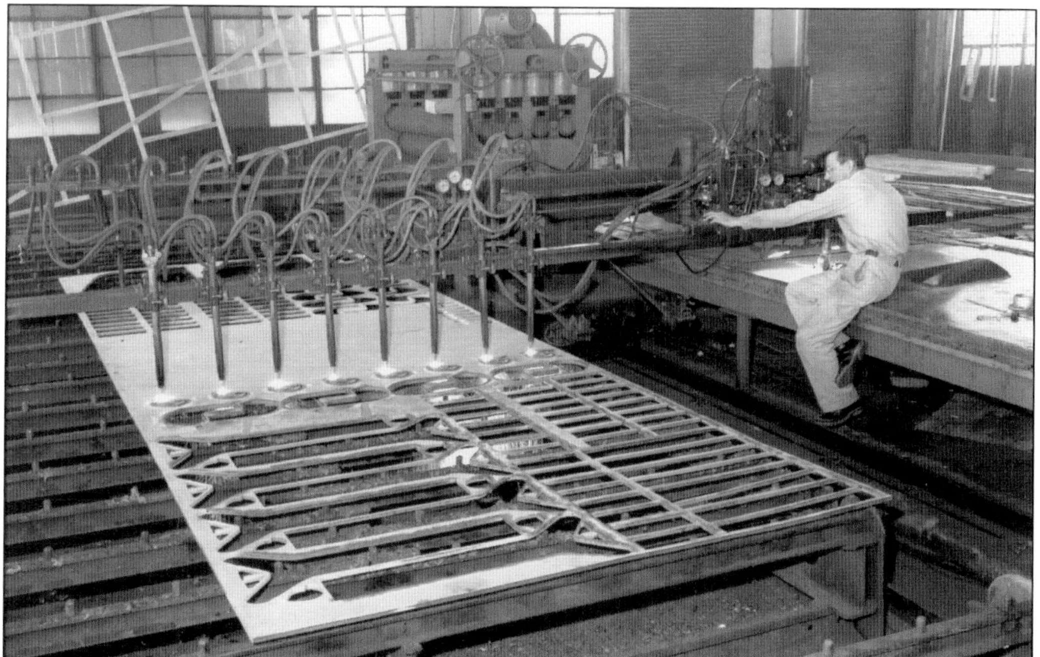

A semi-automated plate cutter at Hardings simultaneously cuts complex shapes from a steel plate with eight torches. Machines such as this one greatly increased efficiency and reduced the amount of difficult and tedious manual labor involved in shipbuilding.

Hardings also did a large amount of non-shipbuilding work in the postwar years. The first big industrial contract was for production of these vending machines—certainly a long way from destroyers. Generally, the industrial contracts were not big moneymakers but covered a share of the overhead costs and kept the workforce busy when shipbuilding activity slowed.

Larger industrial products included rock crushing machinery for Bath subsidiaries Pennsylvania Crusher and Dixie Manufacturing. This huge crusher was actually photographed in the shipyard rather than at Hardings. Postwar industrial work, at Hardings and the main shipyard, was as diverse as wood pulp molding machines, pie plate stamping machines, and of course, Hyde Windlass products after Bath reacquired Hyde in 1961.

The Hardings plant, expanded several times throughout the years, continues its role into the 21st century. All raw steel arrives here by rail and truck and leaves ready for assembly into ship units in the main shipyard. In more recent years, a new warehouse and a pipe and sheetmetal fabrication facility were constructed across the road from Hardings, removing those functions from the main shipyard.

Although Hardings is mostly out of the public view, each ship's construction starts here with an appropriate ceremony. Here, two Navy officers look on as a Bath machine operator cuts a plate during the "start fab" ceremony for the destroyer *Oscar Austin*. The white uniforms are definitely out of place in the industrial environment of a steel fabrication plant.

Bath's other off-site facility, the Portland yard, was built around a former Navy floating drydock. The dock's nine sections were built by four different shipyards in 1943. Bath received the dock after many years in reserve, and it required significant overhaul work before entering service. Three sections are seen, wingwalls folded down, floating in South Boston Drydock No. 3 at the start of the overhaul. (Photograph courtesy Ron Bartlett.)

Known as Advance Base Sectional Dock No. 3 (ABSD 3), the dock was intended to be fully self-sufficient at remote island bases in the Pacific. The pontoons contained full living accommodations for the crew, including this galley, plus all the electrical generation equipment and other machinery necessary to operate the dock. The pontoons and wingwalls also contained a wide variety of workshops, storerooms, offices, and even a barbershop. (Photograph courtesy Ron Bartlett.)

The first ship lifted at Portland was the destroyer *Scott*. The destroyer was damaged in a grounding accident early in 1984, and Portland was the closest facility capable of accommodating the repairs. *Scott* is a big destroyer but is dwarfed by the 744-foot, 81,000-ton capacity drydock. The dock was originally meant to handle ships as large as battleships and aircraft carriers. (Photograph courtesy Ron Bartlett.)

The last ship to use the Portland facility was the new destroyer *Howard*, seen shortly before it undocked on December 15, 2000. *Howard* was in Portland for installation of the sonar dome as well as hull painting prior to sea trials and delivery. In later years, this was Portland's major role, in addition to Post Shakedown Availabilities, a short overhaul and maintenance period several months after a new ship is delivered.

The biggest job undertaken in the Portland drydock was repair of the Bath-built frigate *Samuel B. Roberts* (FFG 58), which had been badly damaged by a mine in the Persian Gulf. The explosion nearly cracked the ship in two and completely destroyed the engine room. The crew managed to save their ship, and *Roberts* was transported to the United States on a heavy lift ship. In this view, the ruined engine room has been cut out in preparation for replacement.

A new engine room unit was fabricated at Bath and taken to Portland on a barge. In this view, a huge floating crane is lowering the new unit into the dock beside the frigate onto a specially designed rail system. It will then be skidded sideways into the void, making the ship whole again. The frigate was placed off-center in the dock to accommodate this operation.

Portland jobs were not exclusively Navy work. Demillo's Floating Restaurant, a converted ferry that has long been a Portland waterfront landmark, received a rebuilt hull in the Portland drydock. A new lower hull was fabricated in the drydock and is approaching completion in this view. The Portland yard had its own set of workshops, but steel assembly on this scale was not typical Portland work.

The restaurant was then floated into the drydock and positioned over the new hull. When the dock was raised, the restaurant came to rest atop the new hull, as seen here. The new and old hulls were then welded together, giving the old restaurant a new lease on life.

The drydock's advanced age and deteriorating condition, a decline in overhaul business, and a decision to consolidate all ship construction operations in Bath, lead to the Portland facility's closure. After the last ship left Portland, the drydock was decommissioned, its cranes dismantled, and set onto the dock floor. In this view, tugs are moving the dock to the pier for the final stages of dismantling. Right up to the end, the dock retained many features left over from World War II, including mounting rings for anti-aircraft guns.

A Croatian shipyard purchased the drydock. It was cut in half and carried across the Atlantic in two trips aboard the heavy lift ship *Blue Marlin*—itself a form of self-propelled floating drydock. *Blue Marlin* is seen here with half the dock lifted, preparing for the long ocean voyage. The old wooden drydock had been taken out of service years earlier and was eventually sold, sinking under tow to its new location.

Eight

Into the Future: Building on the Tradition

In recent years, Bath has finally shed the last historic aspects of shipbuilding, as the traditional shipways were replaced by a modern Land Level Transfer Facility (LLTF)—at last realizing the modernization first planned in the 1960s. The destroyer *Chafee*, the first ship built on the new LLTF, stands fully assembled in this view. Units for the second ship, *Momsen*, are in the foreground awaiting assembly into the hull. These are Bath's 22nd and 23rd *Arleigh Burke*–class guided missile destroyers.

Following the guided missile frigate program, Bath moved on to *Ticonderoga*-class guided missile cruisers, which carry the advanced *Aegis* weapons system. The Bath's first was *Thomas S. Gates* (CG 51), seen in the Portland drydock. The huge, bulbous sonar dome at the bow, which must be installed after launch, demonstrates the need for a drydock. The CGs were designed as replacements for the 1960s frigates (DLGs), many of them Bath-built.

Gates was fitted with two Mk26 missile launchers, firing medium-range anti-aircraft missiles and anti-submarine rockets. In this view, the forward launcher is being tested with a dummy missile as employees and officials look on. *Gates* was the only Bath-built ship to carry this launcher, as subsequent cruisers and destroyers used new vertical-launch missile systems.

Shiloh goes downriver past BIW while Bath's eighth and final cruiser, *Lake Erie*, lies at the finger pier. The big Assembly Building has grown again to a final length of 1,280 feet. The white building on the southern waterfront is the new Preoutfit II building, built on the former Bath Box Company property. The old ways are still in use in this view, with a second heavy crane now in place.

Here are the old and the new—a replica of the 1813 brig *Niagara*, Commodore Oliver Hazard Perry's flagship in the battle of Lake Erie, lies in front of the cruiser *Lake Erie* at the south pier. The guided missile destroyer *Arleigh Burke* (DDG 51), first of the next generation of warships, is to the left. The DDGs are slightly smaller and more modern versions of the cruisers.

A ship unit is being constructed in the Assembly Building. The units are assembled upside down, minimizing the amount of work to be done overhead. At this stage, shipfitters and welders will build the ship's structure, and pipefitters will install larger piping. The unit is then flipped and assembled atop others before being painted.

Arleigh Burke's mast is shown in the Preoutfit II building. In this huge building, the painted units are outfitted with insulation, electronics, wiring, equipment, and other smaller items before going to the ways for assembly into the ship. The mast is the only major aluminum component in a guided missile destroyer, as aluminum superstructures were eliminated after the *Belknap* collision.

The 220-ton capacity No. 11 crane (right) and the new 300-ton No. 15 crane lift the superstructure unit onto a DDG on the ways. The ship's bow lies in the foreground. DDG construction was consolidated to the A- and B-ways, which were flanked by the No. 11 and No. 15 cranes, allowing two-crane lifts. The C-ways, on the other side of No. 11 crane, were abandoned.

Although many things in shipbuilding have changed, the christening has not. Janet Langhart Cohen (left), wife of Secretary of Defense William Cohen, and the Lady Soames, DBE, daughter of Sir Winston Churchill, christen the destroyer *Winston S. Churchill*. More than 8,000 employees and members of the public attended this launch, along with a squadron of American and British dignitaries and military leaders.

The last ship to be launched from the ways, *Mason*, is illuminated by floodlights the night before the June 23, 2001 launch. With this launch, Bath ended the ages-old practice of sliding a ship down the ways in favor of more efficient modern methods. The old launch traditions will be fondly remembered by generations of Bath employees. (Photograph by the author.)

The ways echo with the sounds of wedge driving for the very last time, as employees and guests "wedge up" *Mason* the morning of the ship's launch. Driving wedges in the launch cradle starts the process of transferring the ship's weight onto the cradle and off the blocking, which has supported the ship during construction. The blocking is removed after wedging up, leaving the cradle and ship ready to slide down the greased ways into the river. (Photograph by the author.)

Bath's new drydock comes around Doubling Point Light into Bath after a grueling six-month ocean voyage and a slow five-day trip up the Kennebec. The 750-foot dock is carrying two new cranes for the Land Level Transfer Facility and is towed by the ocean tug *Smitwijs London*, assisted by five smaller tugs. It was the largest structure ever moved on the Kennebec.

Three months after its launching, *Mason* was the first ship to use the new dock. The dock will be used to launch ships built on the LLTF and to lift ships for overhaul and maintenance. *Mason* is viewed between two Outfit Support Towers, permanent steel structures on the LLTF, replacing the semi-temporary staging once used on the ways.

Virginia Chafee (left), widow of the late Senator Chafee, welds her initials on a plaque during the keel laying ceremony for *Chafee* (DDG 90). She is assisted by Bath welder David Gauvin, who will later weld the plaque to the ship. The keel laying ceremony has changed a great deal over the years and would be unrecognizable to those who attended a similar ceremony a century ago. (Photograph by the author.)

Keel laying for *Chafee* involved assembly of four units on the Land Level Transfer Facility. The ship no longer slides on ways. Instead, the units (and eventually the whole ship) roll along a set of rails on a specially built ship transfer system. The unit to the right is rolling into position, while the unit to the upper left is being lowered by an out-of-view crane. (Photograph by the author.)

The completed Land Level Transfer Facility shows the future of Bath Iron Works. The LLTF is a 15-acre facility, built out into the river south of the finger pier. The drydock, which has lifted *Mason* in this view, can move sideways to meet any of the three ship transfer rails and moves into the river to submerge and launch or lift a ship. The inner set of ship rails, where *Chafee* is under construction, is 1,000 feet long and can accommodate two 510-foot destroyers. The outer sets of rails are each 750 feet long. Four sets of crane rails are positioned between the ship rails, and cranes can be swapped between rails as needed. Four cranes serve the facility—the 300-ton No. 15 crane relocated from the old ways, new 300-ton and 100-ton cranes, and a 60-ton crane relocated from Portland. The maximum theoretical unit weight has now reached 600 tons, although the heaviest yet handled is around 500 tons.

The proud crew of *McCampbell* (DDG 85) poses for a photograph aboard the ship, moored outboard of the LLTF just before departure from Bath. The top of a 32-cell vertical launch missile system is barely visible between the superstructure and the 5-inch, 62-caliber gun. The eight-sided panels on the superstructure are two of the four radar faces of the SPY-1 *Aegis* radar system, which eliminates traditional rotating radar antennas.

Painters put the final touches on *Mason* in the new drydock. This view illustrates one major difference between the LLTF-drydock and the ways—equipment can drive right up to the ship, which was never possible on the sloped, crowded ways. This makes it much easier for the workers to do their jobs safely and efficiently.

Despite all the changes in technology and facilities, the skilled workforce is still the most important factor. Equipped with new facilities, crews such as this group posed under *Chafee* on the LLTF can continue Bath's long tradition of building top-quality ships. The men are standing over the ship transfer rails, which will roll the ship into the drydock for launch.

Some aspects of the job are little changed over the years. Here, a crew of stagebuilders is at work high up the mast of *Winston S. Churchill* on Sunday, May 19, 2001. Aside from the modern electronics antennas, this photograph could easily date from a half-century earlier. *Churchill* is back in Bath for Post Shakedown Availability. (Photograph by the author.)

McCampbell, Bath's 20th and most recent guided missile destroyer, is shown on sea trials. Bath's recent past and future are once again centered around destroyers for the Navy. At least 10 more DDGs will follow *McCampbell*, and the DDG program is already the longest-running shipbuilding program in the yard's 119-year history. Ships such as *McCampbell* will be carrying Bath's name and the "Bath-built is best-built" reputation to the front lines around the world for decades to come.